I0161606

CHICAGO
COLORING
BOOK

Please Help Review This Book Here!

Scan For Your Free Coloring Book

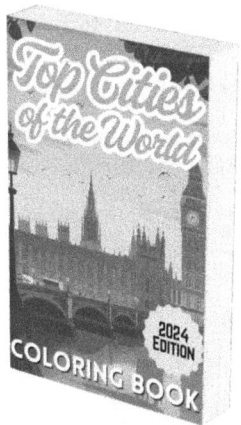

Top Cities of the World

2024 EDITION

COLORING BOOK

CITY LINE PRESS

For permissions, inquiries, or any other requests, please contact: City Line Press at citylinepress@gmail.com. AMDG.

ISBN: 979-8-9887369-4-3 (Paperback)
First Printing Edition 2023

CITY LINE PRESS

WELCOME TO CHICAGO

Location: Chicago is located in the state of Illinois, on the southwestern shore of Lake Michigan.

Nickname: Chicago is often referred to as the "Windy City," a nickname that is believed to have originated from the city's long-winded politicians, rather than its weather.

Population: With a population of over 2.7 million people, Chicago is the third-most populous city in the United States, behind New York City and Los Angeles.

Architecture: Chicago is known for its unique and innovative architecture, with iconic buildings such as the Willis Tower (formerly the Sears Tower) and the John Hancock Center.

Sports: Chicago is home to several professional sports teams, including the Chicago Cubs (MLB), the Chicago White Sox (MLB), the Chicago Bears (NFL), the Chicago Bulls (NBA), and the Chicago Blackhawks (NHL).

Culture: Chicago has a rich cultural scene, with world-class museums, theaters, music venues, and art galleries. The city is particularly known for its blues and jazz music.

Food: Chicago is famous for its food, particularly its deep-dish pizza, Chicago-style hot dogs, and Italian beef sandwiches.

Transportation: Chicago is a major transportation hub, with O'Hare International Airport being one of the busiest airports in the world. The city also has an extensive public transportation system, including the "L" train.

History: Chicago has a storied history, including the Great Chicago Fire of 1871, which destroyed much of the city but led to its rebuilding and growth.

Economy: Chicago is a major financial and business center, with a diverse economy that includes finance, manufacturing, technology, and tourism.

WELCOME TO CHICAGO

10 TALLEST CHICAGO BUILDINGS

1. Willis Tower (formerly Sears Tower)
- Height: 1,451 feet
- Floors: 110
- Completed: 1974
- Description: Iconic skyscraper that once held the title of the tallest building in the world.

2. Trump International Hotel and Tower
- Height: 1,388 feet
- Floors: 98
- Completed: 2009
- Description: Luxury mixed-use tower with stunning views of the Chicago River.

3. St. Regis Chicago
- Height: 1,198 feet
- Floors: 101
- Completed: 2020
- Description: Designed by Jeanne Gang, it's the tallest building by a woman architect.

4. Aon Center
- Height: 1,136 feet
- Floors: 83
- Completed: 1973
- Description: Known for its clean lines and originally clad in white marble.

5. 875 North Michigan Avenue (formerly John Hancock Center)
- Height: 1,127 feet
- Floors: 100
- Completed: 1969
- Description: Features a unique X-braced exterior and an observation deck.

6. Franklin Center (formerly AT&T Corporate Center)
- Height: 1,007 feet
- Floors: 60
- Completed: 1989
- Description: Prominent corporate office building in the Loop.

7. Two Prudential Plaza
- Height: 995 feet
- Floors: 64
- Completed: 1990
- Description: Known for its distinctive slanted roof and spire.

8. One Chicago (East Tower)
- Height: 971 feet
- Floors: 76
- Completed: 2022
- Description: A modern skyscraper featuring luxury residences.

9. 311 South Wacker Drive
- Height: 961 feet
- Floors: 65
- Completed: 1990
- Description: Recognized for its illuminated crown at night.

10. NEMA Chicago
- Height: 896 feet
- Floors: 76
- Completed: 2019
- Description: Chicago's tallest all-residential building with extensive amenities.

HANDCOCK TOWER

CHICAGO PUZZLE

```
F A M M C P R U D E N T I A L O
R K U T P N H O W P F Z J D B J
A V B G T A A J A B J N A Q R O
N N R L V B V C C X O E K J L H
K M O C O K Z P K F Y U A I P N
L T L K V N I V E U O W U O A H
I W R W Q U E W R B M W R J A
N K L U Q P X C F A I X D Q J N
C N W W M N X Z H A O V P L Z C
E G S I Y P H G O I A N H Y S O
N W C L D X T J N X C L M I G C
T W V L K Y X O I E O A G F L K
E A S I D V K K W V M E G K Z O
R R P S A P W C W E R A I O E H
V J P Q D S T J W T R I F W I W
M I E V M U U X S K O X I V V R
```

AON	FRANKLIN CENTER
JOHN HANCOCK	NEMA
ONE CHICAGO	PRUDENTIAL
ST REGIS	TRUMP TOWER
WACKER	WILLIS

TRIBUNE TOWER

DAILY GRATITUDE

I'm Grateful For

1. _____

2. _____

3. _____

4. _____

Today I Feel

This Person or Experience Brought Me Great Joy Today

_____

_____

What was the best part of your day?

SEARS TOWER

TOP CHICAGO FOODS

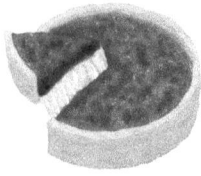

1. Chicago-style Deep Dish Pizza: A thick crust pizza filled with cheese, meat, and tomato sauce, baked in a deep dish pan.

2. Chicago-style Hot Dog: An all-beef hot dog topped with mustard, onions, sweet pickle relish, a dill pickle spear, tomato slices, sport peppers, and a dash of celery salt, served in a poppy seed bun.

3. Italian Beef Sandwich: Thinly sliced roast beef simmered in Italian spices, served on an Italian roll and dipped in the cooking juices.

4. Chicago-style Popcorn: A mix of caramel and cheese popcorn, creating the perfect blend of sweet and savory flavors.

5. Garrett Popcorn: A Chicago institution known for its gourmet popcorn, especially the Garrett Mix, which combines cheese and caramel popcorn.

6. Chicago-style Steak: Indulge in a juicy, well-seasoned steak, often served with potatoes and vegetables.

7. Jibarito: A Puerto Rican sandwich made with flattened, fried plantains instead of bread, filled with meat, cheese, lettuce, and tomatoes.

8. Rainbow Cone: A signature Chicago dessert consisting of five flavors of ice cream (chocolate, strawberry, Palmer House, pistachio, and orange sherbet) stacked on a cone.

9. Chicago-style Pretzel: A large, soft pretzel often served with mustard for dipping.

10. Garlic Shrimp: A popular dish in Chicago's seafood restaurants, featuring shrimp sautéed in garlic butter and served with bread for dipping.

CHICAGO POPCORN

POPCORN

CHICAGO PUZZLE

```
F  R  A  I  N  B  O  W  C  O  N  E  B  O  S  X
U  L  Q  O  S  R  Q  F  L  O  S  I  H  U  T  A
M  D  C  D  M  O  H  Y  H  S  Y  E  C  Z  Q  A
H  D  J  O  E  U  A  O  L  S  T  E  A  K  U  J
O  N  O  Z  G  E  T  V  A  L  E  O  F  V  K  Y
T  F  B  Z  A  I  P  W  C  J  X  L  G  U  T  G
D  V  B  B  R  Z  P  D  T  U  O  Q  R  N  Q  W
O  R  Z  A  R  F  R  S  I  C  Y  U  Z  X  Q  Q
G  L  B  D  E  Y  V  H  Q  S  B  H  D  C  O  J
O  I  I  Z  T  N  Y  R  F  N  H  Q  E  C  C  X
J  D  S  Q  T  A  I  I  P  R  E  T  Z  E  L  S
F  K  D  E  D  K  S  M  H  A  Q  K  J  F  M  E
D  A  Q  L  W  X  Y  P  M  Z  F  W  B  G  U  X
I  T  A  L  I  A  N  B  E  E  F  Q  C  R  Z  A
P  D  H  M  F  I  F  P  O  P  C  O  R  N  G  O
E  K  S  Q  M  M  X  C  S  Y  A  W  X  C  J  C
```

DEEP DISH
HOT DOG
JIBARITO
PRETZEL
SHRIMP

GARRETT
ITALIAN BEEF
POPCORN
RAINBOW CONE
STEAK

CHICAGO DOG

DAILY GRATITUDE

I'm Grateful For

1. _____

2. _____

3. _____

4. _____

Today I Feel

This Person or Experience Brought Me Great Joy Today

_____

_____

What was the best part of your day?

CHICAGO PIZZA

TOP CHICAGO FIRE STATIONS

1. Engine 73 "The Ratdogs": Known for their fierce reputation, lightning-fast responses, and unmatched neighborhood pride, this West Side firehouse is one of Chicago's most iconic companies.

2. Engine 18 / Station 19 (Chicago Fire House from the TV Show): One of the most visited stations in the city thanks to the TV series Chicago Fire, celebrated for its historic architecture and highly skilled crews.

3. Engine 42 (Near North Side): A powerhouse located in the heart of downtown, recognized for protecting some of Chicago's busiest and most high-profile districts.

4. Engine 98 (Water Tower Station): A landmark firehouse beside the historic Water Tower, known for its unique castle-like appearance and deep roots in Chicago firefighting history.

5. Engine 1 / Tower Ladder 10 (Downtown Loop): A frontline unit responsible for the Loop's government buildings, skyscrapers, and dense pedestrian areas—one of the most challenging districts in the city.

6. Engine 55 (Logan Square): Famous for its community outreach, fast responses, and presence in one of Chicago's most vibrant neighborhoods.

7. Engine 13 (West Town): A respected company with decades of experience handling heavy fire activity and dense residential districts.

8. Engine 78 (Wrigleyville): The house that protects Wrigley Field and the bustling sports district, known for crowd-management expertise during Cubs games.

CHICAGO FIRE DEPARTMENT

CHICAGO PUZZLE

```
C O M M U N I T Y I W Y R V D X
X X X U Z X H Z F A V J T J X E
S T X E L X B H I J N T D D O U
S N E I G H B O R H O O D Y C W
Z N G R I Q O K E E P U R I N W
R F V H H U T M H Y A X N C G W
P R K A D V E O O C F O R H S S
C R R Z W G E F U K C D E I N U
C Y O W H N M E S I V O S C K J
U L Y T I I G E E Y U W P A D T
S S M G E O S A W H G N O G U D
M T N Q W C H T S K Z T N O R I
K E F I N P T J O R Y O S V E D
F E P U K H T I N R V W E K O Y
Z M C D W O E K O U I N C X Q B
X K O M F R M N L N K C R X U Z
```

CHICAGO   COMMUNITY
DOWNTOWN   ENGINE
FIREHOUSE   HISTORIC
ICONIC   NEIGHBORHOOD
PROTECTION   RESPONSE

CHICAGO POLICE DEPARTMENT

POLICE

DAILY GRATITUDE

I'm Grateful For

1. _____

2. _____

3. _____

4. _____

Today I Feel

This Person or Experience Brought Me Great Joy Today

_____

_____

What was the best part of your day?

CHICAGO POLICE DEPARTMENT

TOP 10 CHICAGO NEIGHBORHOODS

1. The Loop
- *Vibe*: Business hub with iconic architecture, cultural attractions, and public art.
- *Highlights*: Millennium Park, Willis Tower, Art Institute of Chicago.
- Who it's for: Urban explorers, architecture lovers, and first-time visitors.

2. River North
- *Vibe*: Upscale and trendy with a vibrant nightlife and dining scene.
- *Highlights*: High-end galleries and Chicago Riverwalk.
- Who it's for: Art enthusiasts, foodies, and nightlife seekers.

3. Lincoln Park
- *Vibe*: Leafy and family-friendly with a mix of nature, culture, and history.
- *Highlights*: Lincoln Park Zoo (free), DePaul University, North Avenue Beach.
- Who it's for: Families, nature lovers, and casual strollers.

4. Wicker Park/Bucktown
- *Vibe*: Hip and artistic with boutique shopping and street art.
- *Highlights*: The 606 trail, independent shops, and live music venues.
- Who it's for: Trendsetters, creatives, and young professionals.

5. Old Town
- *Vibe*: Historic charm meets modern living with cobblestone streets and unique shops.
- *Highlights*: Second City comedy club, Old Town Ale House, St. Michael's Church.
- Who it's for: History buffs and entertainment lovers.

6. Pilsen
- *Vibe*: Vibrant and colorful with a strong Mexican-American cultural influence.
- *Highlights*: National Museum of Mexican Art, murals, and authentic tacos.
- Who it's for: Art and food lovers.

7. Hyde Park
- *Vibe*: Intellectual and historic with strong ties to academia.
- *Highlights*: University of Chicago, Museum of Science and Industry, Obama's home.
- Who it's for: History and science buffs.

8. Logan Square
- *Vibe*: Eclectic and bohemian with a growing food and drink scene.
- *Highlights*: Farmers markets, craft breweries, and independent theaters.
- Who it's for: Hipsters, foodies, and laid-back adventurers.

9. Chinatown
- *Vibe*: Lively and immersive with authentic Chinese culture, food, and traditions.
- *Highlights*: Chinatown Gate, Ping Tom Memorial Park, dim sum spots.
- Who it's for: Food enthusiasts and cultural explorers.

10. Andersonville
- *Vibe*: Cozy and community-driven with Swedish roots.
- *Highlights*: Clark Street boutiques, Swedish American Museum.
- Who it's for: Families, boutique shoppers, and food and drink lovers.

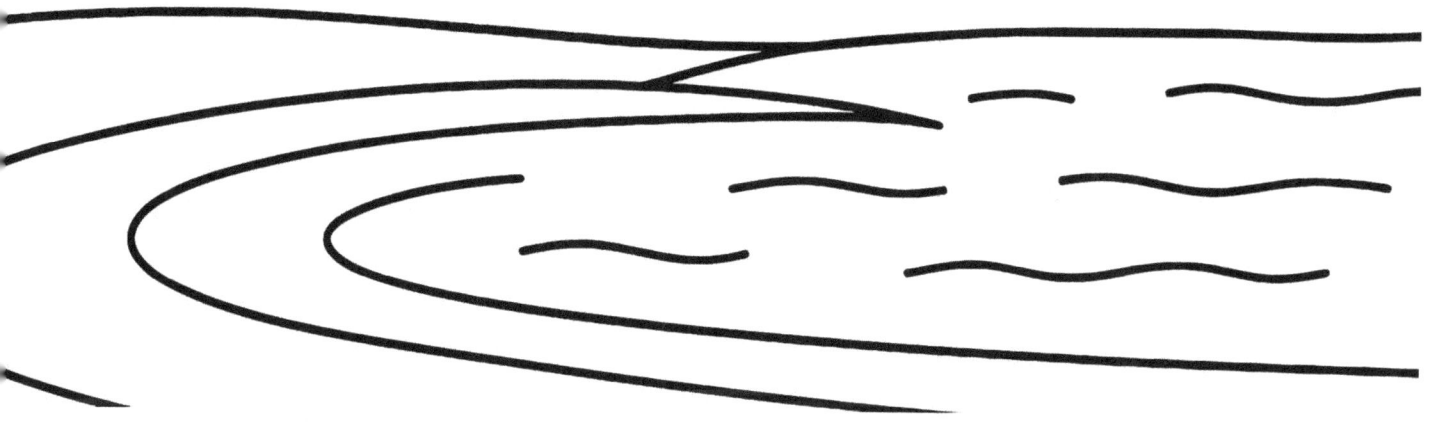

CHICAGO PUZZLE

```
V  A  R  C  P  L  D  N  R  U  G  I  M  K  W  C
I  F  D  E  G  C  R  L  E  C  C  A  S  T  T  E
A  S  E  L  K  E  X  E  M  Q  T  X  T  Q  U  S
T  Y  Q  L  P  S  B  Z  O  P  W  W  A  K  L  Z
O  M  S  P  T  H  C  F  T  K  I  G  K  M  T  R
M  V  I  H  R  M  K  L  E  W  N  A  B  J  I  D
I  Z  L  O  C  B  A  X  R  N  K  S  E  B  C  F
C  R  B  N  W  W  L  E  J  R  I  N  E  H  A  Y
C  M  U  E  P  N  P  O  E  I  E  Y  O  V  T  P
H  C  P  V  D  A  W  X  O  B  S  F  F  E  A  T
A  F  E  R  R  I  S  B  D  D  Y  D  Z  H  L  P
I  C  Y  S  L  S  W  D  H  M  I  Y  U  J  O  A
N  Y  Y  R  O  J  Q  L  Z  X  Z  O  F  A  G  X
I  K  R  S  Z  F  J  E  U  W  B  U  U  X  C  A
S  U  I  O  C  B  T  F  T  X  Z  E  D  A  F  G
T  X  Z  U  S  P  R  A  Y  P  A  I  N  T  R  S
```

ATOMIC CHAIN	BLOOD
CATALOG	CELL PHONE
FERRIS	REMOTE
SKYSRAPER	SPRAY PAINT
TWINKIES	ZIPPER

LINCOLN PARK

DAILY GRATITUDE

I'm Grateful For

1. _____

2. _____

3. _____

4. _____

Today I Feel

This Person or Experience Brought Me Great Joy Today

_____

_____

What was the best part of your day?

GOLD COAST

TOP 10 CHICAGO MUSEUMS

1. Art Institute of Chicago – World-renowned collection, including Nighthawks and A Sunday on La Grande Jatte.

2. Museum of Science and Industry – Interactive exhibits, U-505 submarine, and immersive science displays.

3. Field Museum – Home to "Sue," the largest T. rex skeleton ever discovered.

4. Shedd Aquarium – One of the largest indoor aquariums with an impressive variety of sea life.

5. Adler Planetarium – Hands-on space exhibits and a spectacular view of the skyline.

6. Chicago History Museum – Comprehensive look at Chicago's fascinating past.

7. DuSable Museum of African American History – Dedicated to African American history and culture.

8. Peggy Notebaert Nature Museum – Butterfly Haven and environmental science exhibits.

9. National Museum of Mexican Art – Free museum with rich displays of Mexican culture and art.

10. American Writers Museum – Celebrates American literature and authors in an interactive space.

ART INSTITUTE OF CHICAGO

CHICAGO PUZZLE

```
H C L W A I W H Q E B E B E Y R
S L G Q R E X L D Q X C L M A T
W A R T H P A P E G I B H K M O
I W R I T E R S M D A X W K O C
N H W P Y A Z H W S K D Y F F J
D I X J M X O T U H E S A A F S
Y F P X Z Q U D I W Q F R U I J
C V E I B O C M Z M J J N M W U
I H G G S K W R U N A A B X M F
T I G K X S B H F S C F V S X N
Y S Y F T Y A A G I E Q U C W M
V T O N T A C N X O M U O I J W
S O L J U E D E Z D E F M E O Z
H R C Q B T M L I F X W P N K F
P Y C E J H Y Q E L Q O Z C N A
O A F Y B J R F D R W X N E N H
```

ADLER

DUSABLE

MEXICAN

PEGGY

WINDY CITY

ART

HISTORY

MUSEUM

SCIENCE

WRITERS

ART INSTITUTE OF CHICAGO

DAILY GRATITUDE

I'm Grateful For

1. _____
_____

2. _____
_____

3. _____
_____

4. _____
_____

Today I Feel

This Person or Experience Brought Me Great Joy Today

_____

_____

What was the best part of your day?

FIELD MUSEUM

TOP 10 CHICAGO SPORTS TEAMS

1. Chicago Bears – NFL team known for their strong defense, especially in the 1985 season when they won Super Bowl XX.

2. Chicago Bulls – NBA team famous for their dynasty in the 1990s led by Michael Jordan, winning six championships.

3. Chicago Cubs – MLB team with a long history, known for ending their 108-year championship drought by winning the World Series in 2016.

4. Chicago White Sox – MLB team that won the World Series in 2005, their first championship since 1917.

5. Chicago Blackhawks – NHL team with a storied history, winning three Stanley Cups in the 2010s (2010, 2013, and 2015).

6. Chicago Fire FC – MLS soccer team founded in 1997, named after the Great Chicago Fire, and winners of the MLS Cup in their inaugural season (1998).

7. Chicago Sky – WNBA team that won their first championship in 2021, becoming an important part of Chicago's sports scene.

8. Chicago Red Stars – NWSL soccer team known for developing top female soccer talent and being competitive in the league.

9. Windy City Bulls – NBA G League affiliate of the Chicago Bulls, providing a development pathway for emerging basketball players.

10. Chicago Wolves – AHL hockey team and affiliate of the NHL's Carolina Hurricanes, known for winning multiple league championships.

WRIGLEY FIELD

CHICAGO PUZZLE

```
P R E D S T A R S W Y R H D K U
I J I J M W D I N I M C Y Z A N
N U F Y P Y I X G U U N L E Z W
A X A B R B W N G E F R Y V M Y
U E W Z H N C F D I G P K O C J
W A F F P D U G M Y J J C J J Q
L O C N I L B L X P C Z G G C W
D V L H L R S T A K Y I X N K A
J V O E A E B E A R S T C N N
Q V U S E P V E G K E U B Y J L
T T U C Z S G B F F I I N S M M
Q Q B O J W H I T E S O X L J I
B L A C K H A W K S D U W F C L
T Q F Z B Z Z V T J Q S R S J B
G M P R S L K K Q Q T T Q W X G
F V T B U L L S P C I T Y S V P
```

BEARS
BULLS
FIRE
WHITE SOX
WOLVES

BLACKHAWKS
CUBS
RED STARS
WINDY CITY

COMISKEY PARK

WHITE SOX

DAILY GRATITUDE

I'm Grateful For

1. _____

2. _____

3. _____

4. _____

Today I Feel

This Person or Experience Brought Me Great Joy Today

_____

_____

What was the best part of your day?

SOLDIER FIELD

CHICAGO SPORTS VENUES

Soldier Field – The lakefront colossus where the Monsters of the Midway roared to Super Bowl XX glory in 1985 behind that legendary suffocating defense.

United Center – The Madhouse on Madison, shrine to the 1990s Bulls dynasty where Michael Jordan and six championship banners turned basketball into art.

Wrigley Field – The Friendly Confines on the North Side, century-old cathedral of baseball that finally erupted in joy when the Cubs ended 108 years of heartache with the 2016 World Series.

Guaranteed Rate Field (Comiskey Park) – The South Side armor-clad ballpark where the White Sox shocked the world in 2005, claiming their first title since 1917.

United Center (again, because it's that legendary) – Home of the roaring Blackhawks, where three Stanley Cups were hoisted in the 2010s (2010, 2013, 2015) amid seas of red sweaters and deafening goal horns.

Ryan Field (New Northwestern Stadium) – Evanston's reborn modern fortress, a stunning lakefront arena where college football meets cutting-edge design—built to usher the Wildcats into a new era of Saturday-night roar, purple pride, and Big Ten battles under bright lights.

Wintrust Arena – The sleek South Loop home of the the DePaul Blue Demons and the Chicago Sky, where the franchise captured its first WNBA title in 2021 and cemented its place in the city's championship lore.

Allstate Arena – The Rosemont hockey haven where the Chicago Wolves have piled up Calder Cups and remain the minor-league gold standard while affiliated with Carolina.

UNITED CENTER

CHICAGO PUZZLE

```
T C H A M P I O N S H I P S P S O S
L N O C L X N Y O D S D V R G O
E E X G S Z E D E R K W S L L U
F U O E Z L O E X G J P P H B C
T K K H G C T G E H Y I G A L R
R D Q I R N D T H Y T S B J A I
P E R W A R A M N Y M N O X C M
V W M R I T L U E D A H D A K H
B R A M S N W S O L D I E R H Q
J U M L G N T I N H W L D X A A
G L L U A T L R L Z K S L N W Q
K A N Y N O H D U D Z U Q U K Y
K F R R R I N G J S C M D I S M
R Z R V O E T I L M T A Q L W Y
H B E N B B O E H D Y W T T I I
U L J D K L H H D A U L L S K X
```

ALLSTATE

CHAMPIONSHIPS

RYAN

UNITED

WINTRUST

BLACKHAWKS

GUARANTEED

SOLDIER

WILDCATS

WRIGLEY

RYAN FIELD

RYAN FIELD

NORTHWESTERN

DAILY GRATITUDE

I'm Grateful For

1. _____

2. _____

3. _____

4. _____

Today I Feel

This Person or Experience Brought Me Great Joy Today

_____
_____

What was the best part of your day?

WINTRUST ARENA

TOP CHICAGO UNIVERSITIES

University of Chicago: Elite private research university in Hyde Park, renowned for its ferocious intellectual defense, Nobel Prize dominance, and that legendary undefeated 1985 run in rigorous academics.

Northwestern University: Prestigious private university in Evanston with a dynasty in the 1990s under legendary leadership, capturing six "national championships" in law, journalism, theater, and producing unstoppable GOAT-level alumni (think Michael Jordan, but with briefcases).

Loyola University Chicago: Historic Jesuit university that ended a 108-year "championship drought" in 2016–wait, no, 2018–by winning the NCAA basketball title as the Ramblers, making the whole city believe in miracles again (Cubs energy, but with Sister Jean).

University of Illinois at Chicago (UIC): Scrappy public research university on the Near West Side that shocked the academic world in 2005 with breakthrough research and urban-impact wins after an 88-year wait (White Sox vibes on the South Side? Yes).

DePaul University: The largest Catholic university in the U.S., located in Lincoln Park and known for three straight "Stanley Cup"-level Big East tournament runs in the 2010s while wearing the classic black-and-red colors (basically the Blackhawks of college hoops).

Illinois Institute of Technology (Illinois Tech): STEM-focused university founded in 1997 through merger (but feels reborn after the "Great Chicago Fire" of outdated curricula), winning the national crown in engineering innovation in its very first modern season.

Columbia College Chicago: Creative-arts powerhouse that finally claimed its first national championship in 2021 with an unbeatable film/portfolio season, instantly becoming a major player in the city's cultural scene (Chicago Sky rise, but make it artsy).

Roosevelt University: Social-justice-oriented school in the Loop, consistently developing top-tier talent in public policy, music, and activism while staying fiercely competitive in the national conversation (Red Stars energy).

UNIVERSITY OF CHICAGO

CHICAGO PUZZLE

```
I  H  D  M  L  O  Y  O  L  A  R  P  Z  C  P  V
K  G  U  G  Q  W  K  B  T  E  T  M  U  A  E  V
R  A  O  T  N  C  O  L  U  M  B  I  A  T  L  I
T  I  K  E  R  O  G  O  L  Z  K  N  L  A  F  G
N  A  N  C  O  M  R  U  Z  P  Z  E  Y  P  Z  K
V  V  U  H  Y  F  A  T  R  P  V  A  L  K  U  E
Q  M  U  J  X  P  L  F  H  E  I  Q  F  F  W  J
N  C  K  I  E  W  C  P  S  W  V  G  I  H  I  R
L  S  X  D  C  D  M  O  J  M  E  X  S  G  X  R
P  K  D  S  I  H  O  H  O  A  D  S  K  G  H  V
Z  U  X  P  Y  R  B  G  F  G  K  X  T  M  B  Z
J  J  E  V  Q  M  A  T  Q  I  P  J  T  E  S  R
S  F  C  N  K  C  W  E  U  B  Z  P  N  V  R  L
U  E  N  E  I  A  A  S  F  V  M  H  A  T  L  N
N  V  W  H  D  C  R  T  Z  X  W  K  Z  S  R  G
H  X  C  C  R  E  U  M  U  F  V  P  A  G  B  U
```

CHICAGO	COLUMBIA
DEPAUL	LOYOLA
NORTHWESTERN	ROOSEVELT
TECH	UIC

DEPAUL UNIVERSITY

DEPAUL UNIVERSITY

DAILY GRATITUDE

I'm Grateful For

1. _____

2. _____

3. _____

4. _____

Today I Feel

This Person or Experience Brought Me Great Joy Today

_____

_____

What was the best part of your day?

LOYOLA UNIVERSITY

TOP 10 CHICAGO HIDDEN GEMS

1. Garfield Park Conservatory - Often called "landscape art under glass," this conservatory houses thousands of plant species across eight rooms. Its indoor and outdoor gardens offer a serene escape from the bustling city.

2. Oz Park - This quirky park in Lincoln Park is themed after The Wizard of Oz, featuring sculptures of Dorothy, the Scarecrow, Tin Man, and the Cowardly Lion. It's a delightful spot for families and fans of the classic tale.

3. The Magic Parlour with Dennis Watkins - Located at the historic Palmer House Hotel, this intimate magic show features Dennis Watkins, a third-generation magician. Guests experience close-up illusions in a small, immersive setting.

4. Chicago Pedway System - This network of underground tunnels, ground-level concourses, and overhead bridges connects various parts of downtown Chicago. Perfect for a rainy day, the Pedway reveals a hidden side of the city.

5. National Museum of Mexican Art - Located in Pilsen, this free museum houses one of the most extensive Mexican art collections in the country. It's a vibrant celebration of Mexican culture, with rotating exhibitions, murals, and a fantastic Día de los Muertos celebration.

6. International Museum of Surgical Science - Situated in a historic mansion on Lake Shore Drive, this museum showcases fascinating (and sometimes chilling) exhibits on the history of surgery and medical equipment.

7. Promontory Point - This peaceful spot in Burnham Park offers stunning views of the city skyline across Lake Michigan. It's a favorite spot for locals to picnic, swim, and enjoy sunset views.

8. Peggy Notebaert Nature Museum's Butterfly Haven - This Lincoln Park museum houses a tropical conservatory with hundreds of butterflies, creating an enchanting experience. It's a tranquil escape where you can walk among the fluttering creatures.

9. Henry B. Clarke House - Chicago's oldest house, built in 1836, is a beautifully preserved example of Greek Revival architecture. Located in the Prairie Avenue Historic District, it offers a glimpse into Chicago's early days.

10. Lighthouse Park District at Grosse Point Lighthouse - This historic lighthouse in Evanston (just north of Chicago) offers guided tours and the chance to climb to the top for scenic views. The surrounding gardens and park add to its peaceful charm.

WATER TOWER

CHICAGO PUZZLE

```
L  G  P  L  I  G  H  T  H  O  U  S  E  P  U  B
S  A  T  B  U  T  T  E  R  F  L  Y  K  R  F  F
G  X  O  H  H  E  N  R  Y  C  L  A  R  K  E  F
X  P  L  L  H  M  R  F  V  J  W  E  O  C  N  M
X  M  A  G  I  C  P  A  R  L  O  U  R  G  A  E
W  Z  I  P  C  B  C  U  K  B  D  O  P  H  F  X
O  S  S  Y  K  F  P  E  Z  Y  H  Z  Z  S  N  I
K  K  X  T  M  D  X  Y  Q  C  B  P  P  F  E  C
K  T  O  G  R  N  M  W  J  R  N  A  X  J  X  A
K  Z  N  A  U  J  U  A  V  O  L  R  X  K  H  N
K  U  U  R  L  I  S  I  K  X  J  K  I  F  H  A
B  J  F  F  L  K  E  P  O  I  N  T  Y  H  P  R
Y  J  Q  I  L  H  U  L  H  J  E  G  K  H  G  T
U  L  F  E  K  B  M  C  B  P  E  D  W  A  Y  X
Z  O  M  L  E  G  X  A  Y  T  F  Z  U  C  P  V
K  A  L  D  Y  J  B  B  Q  K  N  L  Y  M  E  X
```

BUTTERFLY	GARFIELD
HENRY CLARKE	LIGHTHOUSE
MAGIC PARLOUR	MEXICAN ART
MUSEUM	OZ PARK
PEDWAY	POINT

CHICAGO BEAN

DAILY GRATITUDE

I'm Grateful For

1. _____

2. _____

3. _____

4. _____

Today I Feel

This Person or Experience Brought Me Great Joy Today

_____

_____

What was the best part of your day?

MUSEUM OF SCIENCE AND INDUSTRY

TOP SCIENCE & NATURE PLACES

The Field Museum – The lakefront titan where ancient defenses stand eternal, home to Sue the T. rex and the unbreakable 1985-level dominance of natural history collections that crushed the competition and claimed the crown of the world's greatest dinosaur exhibits.

Adler Planetarium – America's first planetarium, the cosmic dynasty of the 1990s era (and beyond), where visitors witnessed six mind-blowing sky shows under the dome and still orbit around the legacy of astronomical greatness.

Shedd Aquarium – The beloved North Side classic with a century-plus of history, finally ending a 108-year beluga-whale-sized drought in 2016 when the stunning Oceanarium renovations and the birth of baby Pacific white-sided dolphins made the whole city believe in aquatic miracles again.

Museum of Science and Industry – The South Side powerhouse in the last palace of the 1893 World's Fair, delivering a shocking U-505 submarine capture and coal-mine-to-space breakthrough in 2005 after decades of waiting for that next-level interactive title.

Lincoln Park Zoo – America's free-admission urban wildlife dynasty, hoisting three "Stanley Cup" moments of conservation triumph in the 2010s with the birth of western lowland gorilla troops, red ape breakthroughs, and polar bear royalty amid roaring crowds of red-shirted families.

Peggy Notebaert Nature Museum – Born from the ashes of the Chicago Academy of Sciences' original collection lost in the Great Fire of 1871, reborn in 1997 and winning the "MLS Cup" of public nature education in its inaugural modern season with the iconic Judy Istock Butterfly Haven.

Jackson Park's Garden of the Phoenix and the surrounding Wooded Island – The serene South Side oasis that soared to its first championship-level beauty in 2021 with the full restoration of the historic Japanese garden, instantly becoming one of the city's most peaceful and photogenic natural escapes.

Northerly Island – The reclaimed peninsula and former airport turned 120-acre prairie and migratory-bird sanctuary, consistently developing world-class habitat for rare species while staying fiercely competitive on every Midwest birding Big Day list.

Morton Arboretum – The 1,700-acre living laboratory out in suburban Lisle (but forever part of greater Chicagoland), the NBA G-League affiliate of tree science that grooms future botanical superstars before they get called up to the big research leagues.

Brookfield Zoo Chicago – The sprawling west-suburban wildlife powerhouse and affiliate of global conservation giants, racking up multiple "Calder Cup"-style breeding successes with dolphins, gorillas, and Mexican gray wolves while quietly dominating behind-the-scenes species survival plans.

ADLER PLANETARIUM

CHICAGO PUZZLE

```
E  E  N  O  T  E  B  A  E  R  T  N  M  R  S  D
F  R  T  Q  C  M  N  D  P  L  Q  V  X  S  U  H
U  B  Y  F  U  E  D  O  N  P  N  U  I  P  P  G
R  R  E  V  P  E  E  L  R  I  E  D  X  J  N  K
F  O  A  B  H  H  O  M  S  T  J  B  G  R  G  N
H  O  Y  S  P  C  Z  M  O  E  H  Q  O  W  F  X
M  K  B  F  N  L  A  W  W  R  K  E  O  J  L  H
I  F  L  I  I  V  I  Y  A  O  T  L  R  X  L  X
C  I  L  H  G  E  T  B  L  Y  D  O  U  L  I  K
N  E  T  M  T  R  L  R  F  L  S  S  N  N  Y  C
H  L  F  C  E  U  C  D  A  J  O  Q  E  D  H  M
W  D  J  L  I  Z  T  W  V  C  Q  O  Q  L  X  Z
M  U  D  Q  C  R  L  C  Q  B  H  Q  W  V  V  K
V  A  C  Z  U  K  K  E  R  P  V  S  A  L  J  G
K  M  W  Y  K  D  U  O  B  H  P  N  T  V  H  A
B  X  F  K  R  W  Q  S  J  M  R  V  L  M  Z  B
```

ADLER
FIELD
MORTON
NORTHERLY
PHOENIX

BROOKFIELD
LINCOLN
MSI
NOTEBAERT
SHEDD

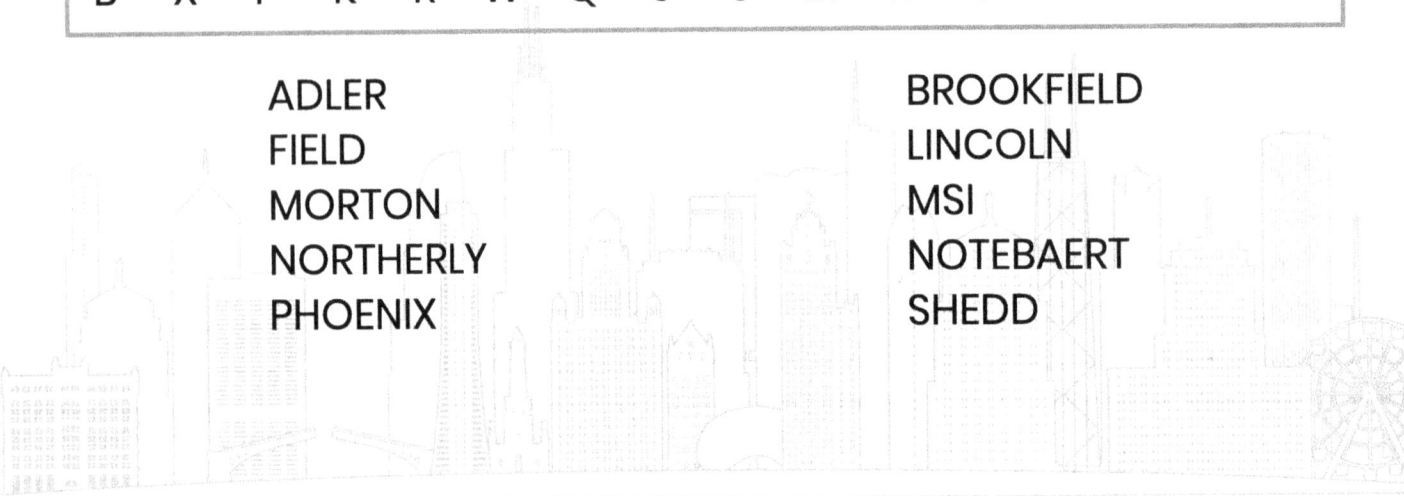

SHEDD AQUARIUM

SHEDD AQUARIUM

DAILY GRATITUDE

I'm Grateful For

1. _____

2. _____

3. _____

4. _____

Today I Feel

☺ ☹ 😠 😟 😆 🤒

This Person or Experience Brought Me Great Joy Today

_____
_____

What was the best part of your day?

TOP 10 CHICAGO EVENTS

1. Chicago Marathon- Held every October, this world-renowned marathon attracts runners from around the globe to traverse the city's diverse neighborhoods.

2. Taste of Chicago - Recognized as the world's largest food festival, it offers a smorgasbord of culinary experiences in Grant Park, featuring food from the city's top restaurants, live music, and family-friendly activities.

3. Chicago Air and Water Show- Every August, this free event showcases daredevil pilots, parachute teams, and formation jet flyers over Lake Michigan, attracting millions of spectators.

4. Chicago Blues Festival- Celebrating the city's rich blues heritage, this June festival in Millennium Park features performances by renowned blues musicians.

5. Chicago Jazz Festival- Held annually in late summer, this festival showcases both legendary and emerging jazz artists in Millennium Park.

6. St. Patrick's Day Parade and River Dyeing- In March, Chicago celebrates St. Patrick's Day by dyeing the Chicago River green, followed by a festive parade through downtown.

7. Chinese New Year Parade- Celebrated in February, this event in Chinatown features traditional dragon and lion dances, colorful floats, and cultural performances to ring in the Lunar New Year.

8. Magnificent Mile Lights Festival- Kicking off the holiday season in November, this festival features a tree-lighting parade along Michigan Avenue, culminating in a fireworks display over the Chicago River.

9. Chicago Thanksgiving Parade- Taking place on State Street, this parade features floats, marching bands, and balloons, kicking off the holiday season.

10. Lollapalooza- This four-day music festival in Grant Park, typically held in late July or early August, features a diverse lineup of artists across multiple genres.

AIR & WATER SHOW

CHICAGO PUZZLE

```
U  I  U  V  E  Z  P  O  E  R  R  A  B  E  H  H
P  W  H  V  Z  W  S  P  G  K  Z  G  H  K  O  N
G  M  R  A  I  A  Q  J  H  O  W  J  C  G  O  R
G  Q  J  I  H  U  I  H  O  C  Z  I  A  H  X  T
A  K  C  G  U  F  I  L  A  E  R  C  T  D  Q  H
D  L  R  N  Y  X  A  P  C  T  I  A  I  S  I  A
U  P  Q  R  R  P  T  P  A  H  R  U  Q  S  P  N
Q  X  F  V  A  X  S  P  C  A  V  J  C  E  L  K
N  T  K  L  R  Z  T  F  M  T  P  W  H  U  Z  S
P  B  L  U  E  S  O  O  T  T  O  Z  I  V  O  G
N  O  C  Q  A  E  G  I  J  H  A  F  N  G  D  I
L  L  E  L  T  A  V  M  S  F  C  W  E  S  H  V
Z  B  K  S  C  Y  Y  R  B  S  U  J  S  Z  H  I
C  H  A  I  O  U  I  F  M  I  Z  O  E  U  U  N
Z  T  H  M  P  A  P  Z  P  J  Q  E  G  G  G  G
H  C  Q  M  Z  R  N  P  A  Z  O  X  E  C  C  L
```

AIR SHOW

CHICAGO MARATHON

JAZZ

ST PATRICK

THANKSGIVING

BLUES

CHINESE

LOLLAPALOOZA

TASTE OF CHICAGO

DAILY GRATITUDE

I'm Grateful For

1. _____

2. _____

3. _____

4. _____

Today I Feel

😊 ☹️ 😠 😕 😆 🤒

This Person or Experience Brought Me Great Joy Today

_____

_____

What was the best part of your day?

CHICAGO INVENTIONS

TOP 10 CHICAGO INVENTIONS

1. Skyscraper – Chicago is the birthplace of the modern skyscraper, with the Home Insurance Building (1885) being the first steel-framed high-rise building.

2. Ferris Wheel – Invented by George Washington Gale Ferris Jr. for the 1893 World's Columbian Exposition in Chicago, it became an amusement park staple worldwide.

3. Cell Phone – The first mobile phone call was made by Martin Cooper of Motorola, headquartered in the Chicago area, in 1973.

4. Television Remote Control – Zenith Electronics, based in Chicago, developed the first wireless remote control for television in the 1950s, changing home entertainment.

5. Spray Paint – Invented in 1949 by Edward Seymour in the Chicago area, spray paint revolutionized painting and graffiti art.

6. Mail-Order Catalog – Chicago-based Montgomery Ward created the first mail-order catalog in 1872, transforming retail and shopping practices.

7. Blood Bank – Dr. Bernard Fantus, from Cook County Hospital in Chicago, established the first blood bank in 1937, revolutionizing healthcare and emergency medicine.

8. Atomic Chain Reaction – The world's first controlled nuclear chain reaction was achieved in 1942 by Enrico Fermi and his team at the University of Chicago, initiating the atomic age.

9. Twinkies – Invented in 1930 by James Dewar of the Chicago-based Hostess company, Twinkies became an iconic American snack.

10. Zipper – Though it had been conceptualized earlier, the modern zipper was perfected and manufactured on a large scale in Chicago by Gideon Sundback and the Universal Fastener Company.

CHICAGO INVENTIONS

CHICAGO PUZZLE

```
V A R C P L D N R U G I M K W C
I F D E G C R L E C C A S T T E
A S E L K E X E M Q T X T Q U S
T Y Q L P S B Z O P W W A K L Z
O M S P T H C F T K I G K M T R
M V I H R M K L E W N A B J I D
I Z L O C B A X R N K S E B C F
C R B N W W L E J R I N E H A Y
C M U E P N P O E I E Y O V T P
H C P V D A W X O B S F F E A T
A F E R R I S B D D Y D Z H L P
I C Y S L S W D H M I Y U J O A
N Y Y R O J Q L Z X Z O F A G X
I K R S Z F J E U W B U U X C A
S U I O C B T F T X Z E D A F G
T X Z U S P R A Y P A I N T R S
```

ATOMIC CHAIN
CATALOG
FERRIS
SKYSRAPER
TWINKIES

BLOOD
CELL PHONE
REMOTE
SPRAY PAINT
ZIPPER

CHICAGO INVENTIONS

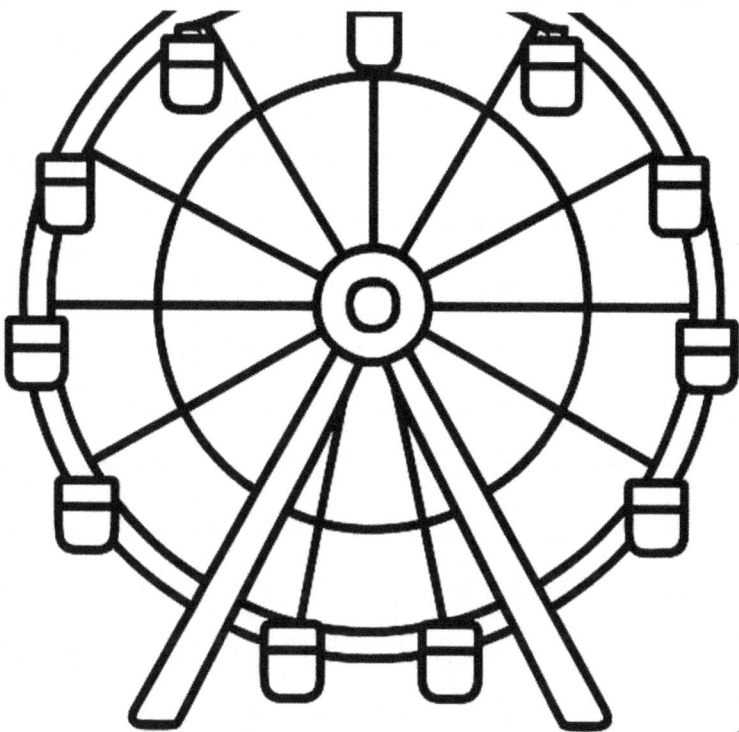

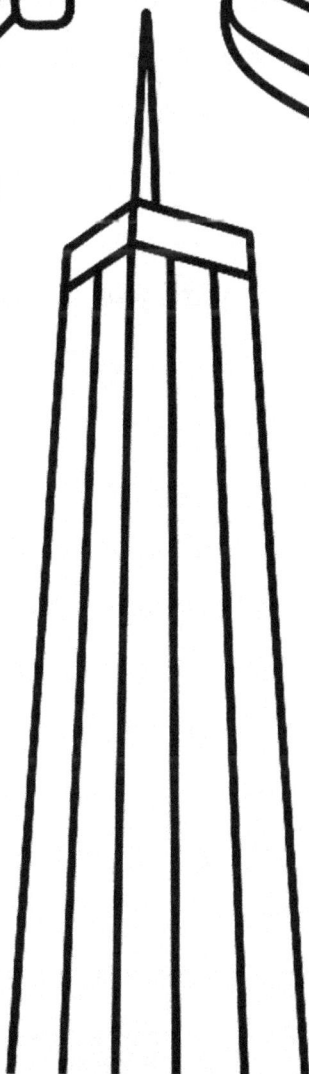

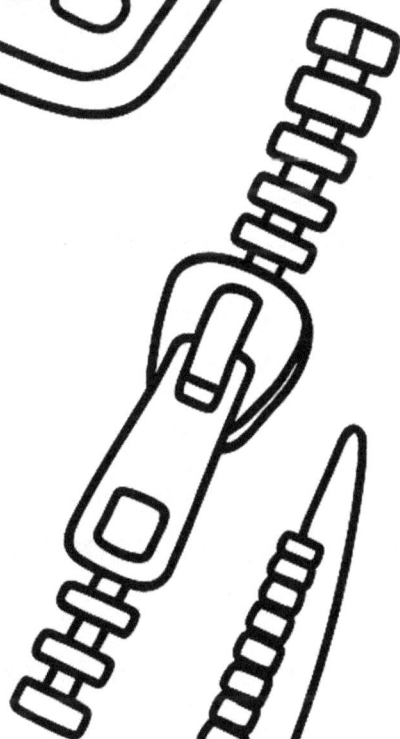

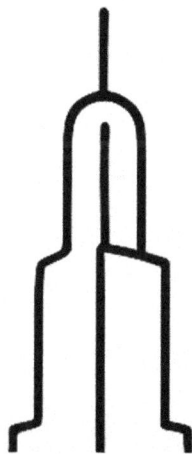

Twinkie

DAILY GRATITUDE

I'm Grateful For

1. _____

2. _____

3. _____

4. _____

Today I Feel

This Person or Experience Brought Me Great Joy Today

_____

_____

What was the best part of your day?

PICASSO STATUE

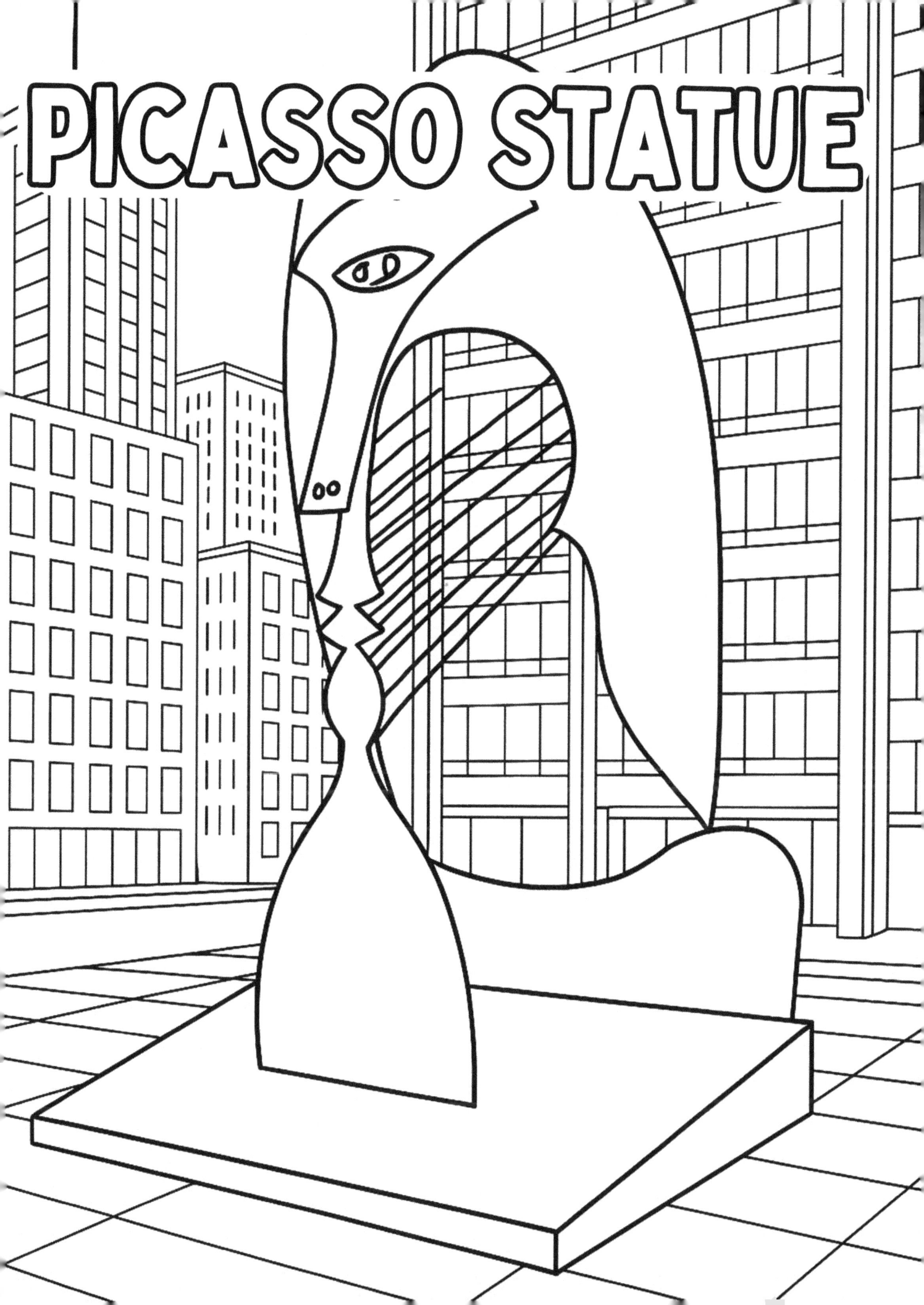

TOP 10 PUBLIC ART IN CHICAGO

1. Cloud Gate (The Bean) – Iconic mirrored sculpture in Millennium Park.

2. Crown Fountain – Digital art fountain with interactive video in Millennium Park.

3. Flamingo by Alexander Calder – Large red sculpture in the Federal Plaza.

4. Picasso Sculpture – Massive, untitled sculpture in Daley Plaza.

5. Agora Sculptures – Array of giant, headless figures in Grant Park.

6. Four Seasons by Marc Chagall – Mosaic mural at Chase Tower Plaza.

7. Miro's Chicago – Abstract sculpture by Joan Miró outside the Chicago Temple.

8. Monument with Standing Beast by Jean Dubuffet – Black and white sculpture at the Thompson Center.

9. Fountain of the Great Lakes – Classic bronze sculpture at the Art Institute of Chicago.

10. Moose Bubblegum Bubble – Whimsical street art mural of a moose blowing a bubble.

BUCKINGHAM FOUNTAIN

CHICAGO PUZZLE

```
Z O F O U R S E A S O N S T L T
I X W Y W R E O E S B K L M N O
E M C X J M N W Z X Y P Q O B W
U O X Y D I I L P N J E G O J A
S N H H A O X R N B R N D S K F
R U N I D S O K O H I F C E U G
N M I T S S I N P M T W A U B W
P E R Q S W R O A G J T L M V H
I N D A T Y Z L A A E N H D V C
K T C G M H F L Y G W E Q M H U
P I G F G D E E S O O T I W V F
P N K P I B P B R O G R N V W L
H K A Q Y A N C E F K K A J E G
C E L L N B J I E A A N D W L D
N N A H Q V T H C P N R R Z C Q
L J G T O S F O U N T A I N S D
```

AGORA	CROWN
FLAMINGO	FOUNTAIN
FOUR SEASONS	MIRO
MONUMENT	MOOSE
PICASSO	THE BEAN

CLOUD GATE

DAILY GRATITUDE

I'm Grateful For

1. _____

2. _____

3. _____

4. _____

Today I Feel

This Person or Experience Brought Me Great Joy Today

_____

_____

What was the best part of your day?

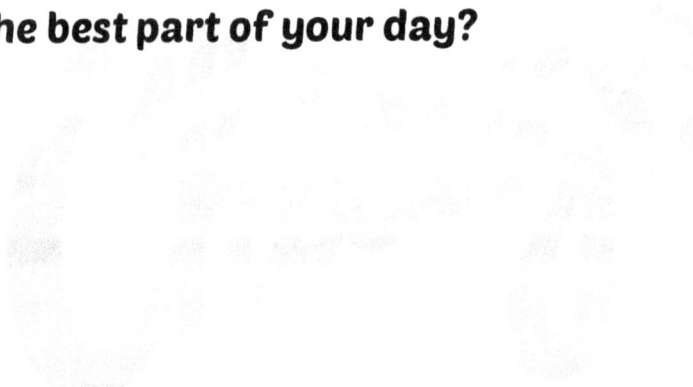

Chicago

We hope you are enjoying this book!

We greatly appreciate the time you took to explore this travel journal. As a small publisher, it means a lot and we hope we are making your travels fun and memorable.

If you have 60 seconds, it would mean the world to us to hear your honest feedback on Amazon.

To leave your feedback:

1. **Open your camera app**
2. **Point your mobile device on the QR code below**
3. **The review page will appear in your web browser**

TOP 10 CHICAGO NEIGHBORHOODS

1. The Loop
- *Vibe*: Business hub with iconic architecture, cultural attractions, and public art.
- *Highlights*: Millennium Park, Willis Tower, Art Institute of Chicago.
- Who it's for: Urban explorers, architecture lovers, and first-time visitors.

2. River North
- *Vibe*: Upscale and trendy with a vibrant nightlife and dining scene.
- *Highlights*: High-end galleries and Chicago Riverwalk.
- Who it's for: Art enthusiasts, foodies, and nightlife seekers.

3. Lincoln Park
- *Vibe*: Leafy and family-friendly with a mix of nature, culture, and history.
- *Highlights*: Lincoln Park Zoo (free), DePaul University, North Avenue Beach.
- Who it's for: Families, nature lovers, and casual strollers.

4. Wicker Park/Bucktown
- *Vibe*: Hip and artistic with boutique shopping and street art.
- *Highlights*: The 606 trail, independent shops, and live music venues.
- Who it's for: Trendsetters, creatives, and young professionals.

5. Old Town
- *Vibe*: Historic charm meets modern living with cobblestone streets and unique shops.
- *Highlights*: Second City comedy club, Old Town Ale House, St. Michael's Church.
- Who it's for: History buffs and entertainment lovers.

6. Pilsen
- *Vibe*: Vibrant and colorful with a strong Mexican-American cultural influence.
- *Highlights*: National Museum of Mexican Art, murals, and authentic tacos.
- Who it's for: Art and food lovers.

7. Hyde Park
- *Vibe*: Intellectual and historic with strong ties to academia.
- *Highlights*: University of Chicago, Museum of Science and Industry, Obama's home.
- Who it's for: History and science buffs.

8. Logan Square
- *Vibe*: Eclectic and bohemian with a growing food and drink scene.
- *Highlights*: Farmers markets, craft breweries, and independent theaters.
- Who it's for: Hipsters, foodies, and laid-back adventurers.

9. Chinatown
- *Vibe*: Lively and immersive with authentic Chinese culture, food, and traditions.
- *Highlights*: Chinatown Gate, Ping Tom Memorial Park, dim sum spots.
- Who it's for: Food enthusiasts and cultural explorers.

10. Andersonville
- *Vibe*: Cozy and community-driven with Swedish roots.
- *Highlights*: Clark Street boutiques, Swedish American Museum.
- Who it's for: Families, boutique shoppers, and food and drink lovers.

GRANT PARK

CHICAGO PUZZLE

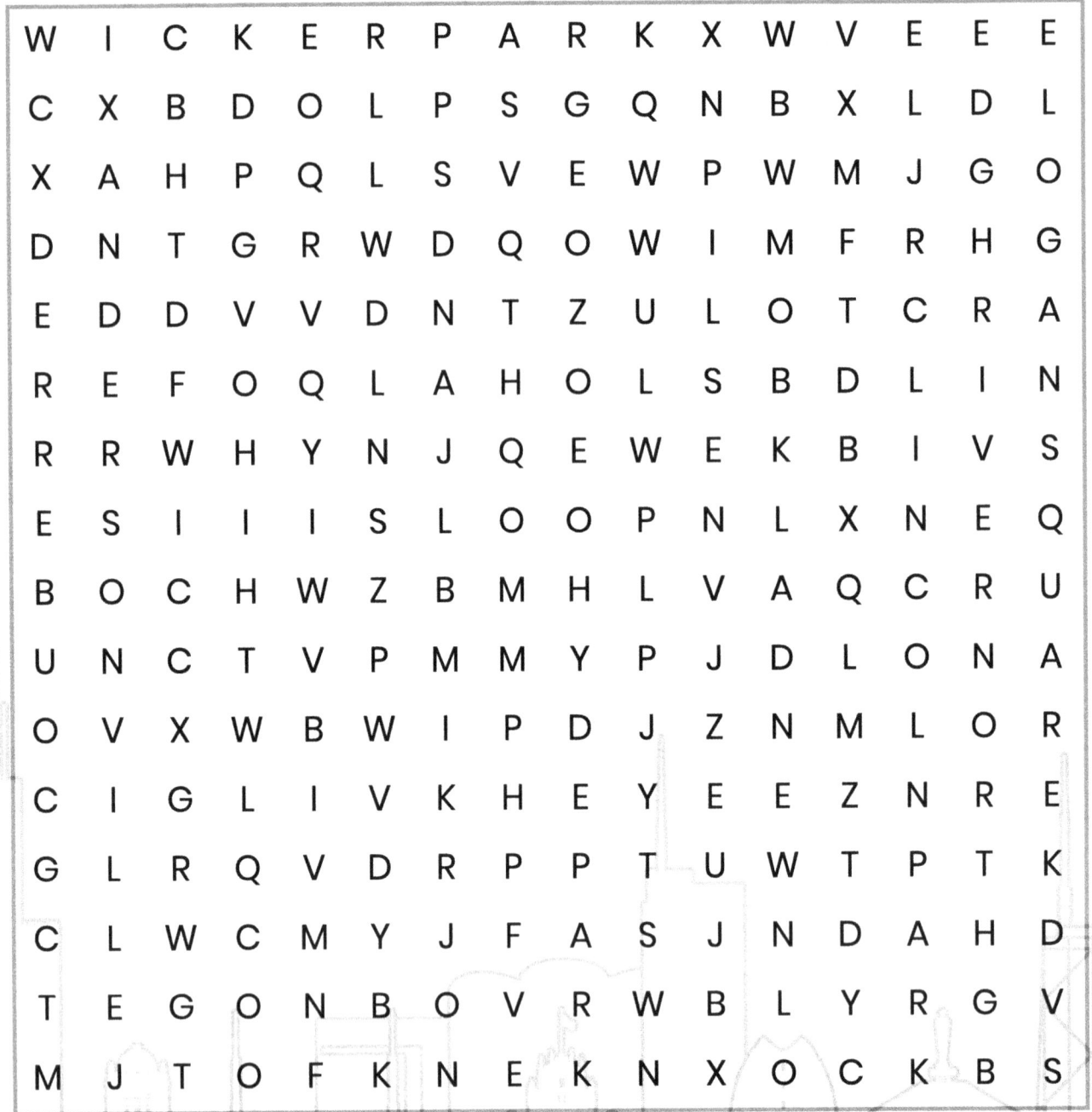

```
W  I  C  K  E  R  P  A  R  K  X  W  V  E  E  E
C  X  B  D  O  L  P  S  G  Q  N  B  X  L  D  L
X  A  H  P  Q  L  S  V  E  W  P  W  M  J  G  O
D  N  T  G  R  W  D  Q  O  W  I  M  F  R  H  G
E  D  D  V  V  D  N  T  Z  U  L  O  T  C  R  A
R  E  F  O  Q  L  A  H  O  L  S  B  D  L  I  N
R  R  W  H  Y  N  J  Q  E  W  E  K  B  I  V  S
E  S  I  I  I  S  L  O  O  P  N  L  X  N  E  Q
B  O  C  H  W  Z  B  M  H  L  V  A  Q  C  R  U
U  N  C  T  V  P  M  M  Y  P  J  D  L  O  N  A
O  V  X  W  B  W  I  P  D  J  Z  N  M  L  O  R
C  I  G  L  I  V  K  H  E  Y  E  E  Z  N  R  E
G  L  R  Q  V  D  R  P  P  T  U  W  T  P  T  K
C  L  W  C  M  Y  J  F  A  S  J  N  D  A  H  D
T  E  G  O  N  B  O  V  R  W  B  L  Y  R  G  V
M  J  T  O  F  K  N  E  K  N  X  O  C  K  B  S
```

ANDERSONVILLE   CHINATOWN
HYDE PARK   LINCOLN PARK
LOGAN SQUARE   LOOP
OLD TOWN   PILSEN
RIVER NORTH   WICKER PARK

DAILY GRATITUDE

I'm Grateful For

1. _____

2. _____

3. _____

4. _____

Today I Feel

This Person or Experience Brought Me Great Joy Today

_____
_____

What was the best part of your day?

PILSEN

FAMOUS CHICAGOANS

1. Barack Obama
- **Vibe: Visionary leader with deep community roots and global influence.**
- **Highlights: Former U.S. President, taught at the University of Chicago, launched his career on the South Side.**

2. Oprah Winfrey
- **Vibe: Media royalty who transformed Chicago into the capital of talk television.**
- **Highlights: The Oprah Winfrey Show, Harpo Studios, philanthropic impact across the city.**

3. Michael Jordan
- **Vibe: The GOAT of basketball, synonymous with Chicago excellence and competitive fire.**
- **Highlights: Six NBA championships with the Bulls, the United Center statue, global icon.**

4. Kanye West
- **Vibe: Creative genius and trendsetter with deep South Side origins.**
- **Highlights: Groundbreaking albums, cultural influence, and Chicago-themed work like "Homecoming."**

5. Michelle Obama
- **Vibe: Grace, intellect, and South Side pride.**
- **Highlights: Princeton and Harvard alum, former First Lady, advocate for education and wellness.**

6. Chance the Rapper
- **Vibe: Modern Chicago storyteller blending activism, positivity, and independent artistry.**
- **Highlights: Grammy wins, community philanthropy, iconic Chicago references in his music.**

7. Robin Williams
- **Vibe: Whimsical comedic genius born with Chicago roots.**
- **Highlights: Legendary stand-up career, unforgettable film performances.**

8. Jennifer Hudson
- **Vibe: Vocal powerhouse rising from Chicago to EGOT status.**
- **Highlights: Dreamgirls, American Idol, award-winning performances.**

9. Harrison Ford
- **Vibe: Rugged Chicago-born star whose characters defined adventure cinema.**
- **Highlights: Star Wars, Indiana Jones, decades-long Hollywood legacy.**

10. Muddy Waters
- **Vibe: The godfather of Chicago blues, electrifying American music forever.**
- **Highlights: Chicago Blues Scene, Chess Records, influence on rock legends.**

FAMOUS
CHICAGOANS

BULLS

CHICAGO PUZZLE

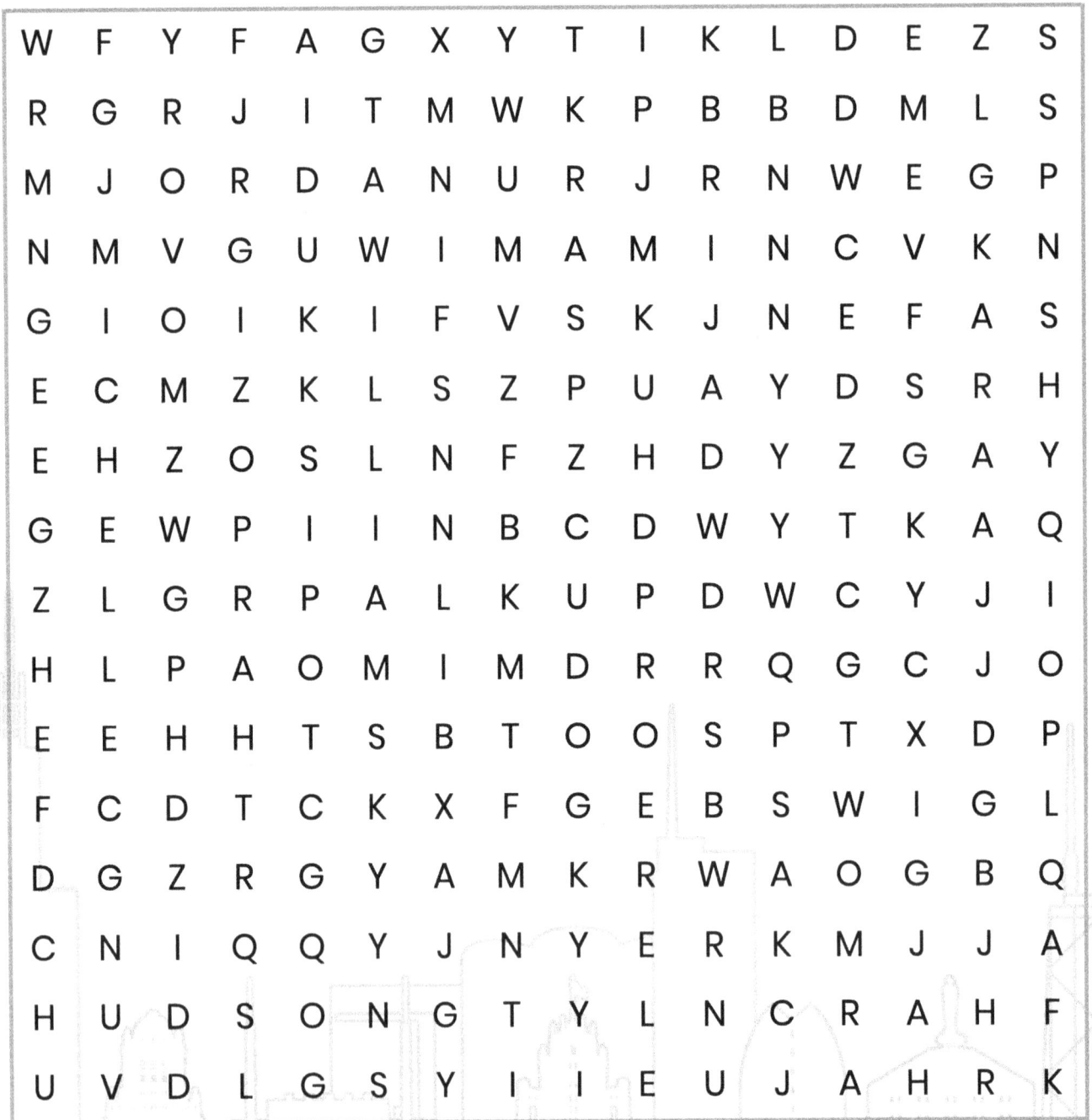

```
W F Y F A G X Y T I K L D E Z S
R G R J I T M W K P B B D M L S
M J O R D A N U R J R N W E G P
N M V G U W I M A M I N C V K N
G I O I K I F V S K J N E F A S
E C M Z K L S Z P U A Y D S R H
E H Z O S L N F Z H D Y Z G A Y
G E W P I I N B C D W Y T K A Q
Z L G R P A L K U P D W C Y J I
H L P A O M I M D R R Q G C J O
E E H H T S B T O O S P T X D P
F C D T C K X F G E B S W I G L
D G Z R G Y A M K R W A O G B Q
C N I Q Q Y J N Y E R K M J J A
H U D S O N G T Y L N C R A H F
U V D L G S Y I I E U J A H R K
```

CHANCE	FORD
HUDSON	JORDAN
KANYE	MICHELLE
MUDDY	OBAMA
OPRAH	WILLIAMS

DAILY GRATITUDE

I'm Grateful For

1. _____

2. _____

3. _____

4. _____

Today I Feel

This Person or Experience Brought Me Great Joy Today

_____

_____

What was the best part of your day?

OBAMA LIBRARY

DAILY GRATITUDE

I'm Grateful For

1. _____

2. _____

3. _____

4. _____

Today I Feel

This Person or Experience Brought Me Great Joy Today

_____

_____

What was the best part of your day?

LINCOLN PARK ZOO

DAILY GRATITUDE

I'm Grateful For

1. _____

2. _____

3. _____

4. _____

Today I Feel

This Person or Experience Brought Me Great Joy Today

_____

_____

What was the best part of your day?

CHICAGO 'L' TRAIN

DAILY GRATITUDE

I'm Grateful For

1. _____

2. _____

3. _____

4. _____

Today I Feel

This Person or Experience Brought Me Great Joy Today

_____

_____

What was the best part of your day?

DAILY GRATITUDE

I'm Grateful For

1. _____

2. _____

3. _____

4. _____

Today I Feel

This Person or Experience Brought Me Great Joy Today

_____

_____

What was the best part of your day?

CHICAGO WINTER

CHICAGO

DAILY GRATITUDE

I'm Grateful For

1. _____

2. _____

3. _____

4. _____

Today I Feel

😊 ☹️ 😠 😔 😆 🤒

This Person or Experience Brought Me Great Joy Today

_____
_____

What was the best part of your day?

THE PLAY PEN

DAILY GRATITUDE

I'm Grateful For

1. _____

2. _____

3. _____

4. _____

Today I Feel

This Person or Experience Brought Me Great Joy Today

_____

_____

What was the best part of your day?

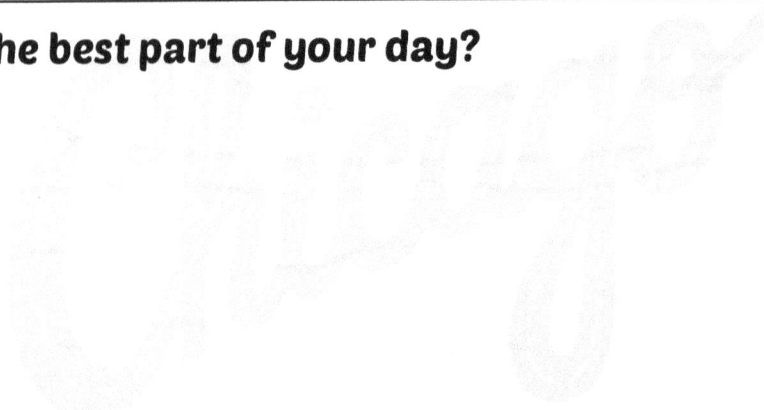

GARFIELD PARK CONSERVATORY

DAILY GRATITUDE

I'm Grateful For

1. _____

2. _____

3. _____

4. _____

Today I Feel

This Person or Experience Brought Me Great Joy Today

_____

_____

What was the best part of your day?

TASTE OF CHICAGO

TASTE OF CHICAGO

FOOD

DAILY GRATITUDE

I'm Grateful For

1. _____

2. _____

3. _____

4. _____

Today I Feel

☺ ☹ 😠 😔 😆 😕

This Person or Experience Brought Me Great Joy Today

_____

_____

What was the best part of your day?

CHICAGO BLIZZARD

CHICAGO

DAILY GRATITUDE

I'm Grateful For

1. _____

2. _____

3. _____

4. _____

Today I Feel

This Person or Experience Brought Me Great Joy Today

_____
_____

What was the best part of your day?

HOLY NAME CATHEDRAL

DAILY GRATITUDE

I'm Grateful For

1. _____

2. _____

3. _____

4. _____

Today I Feel

☺ ☹ 😠 😟 😆 🤒

This Person or Experience Brought Me Great Joy Today

_____

_____

What was the best part of your day?

NAVY PIER

NAVY PIER

PUZZLE ANSWERS

PUZZLE ANSWERS

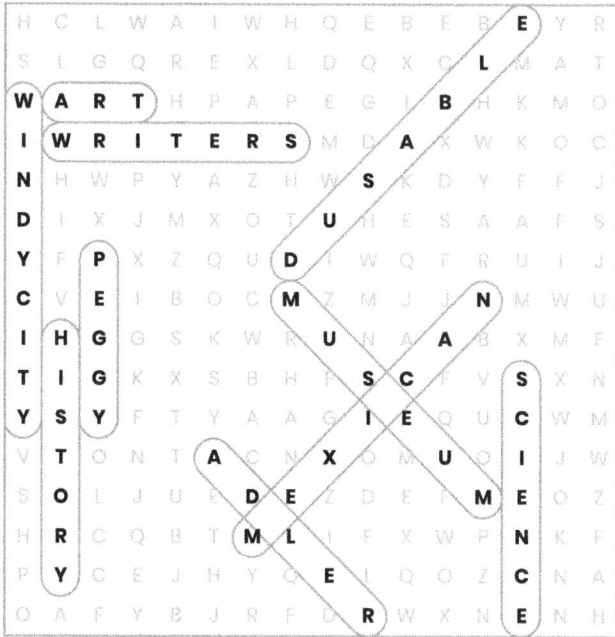

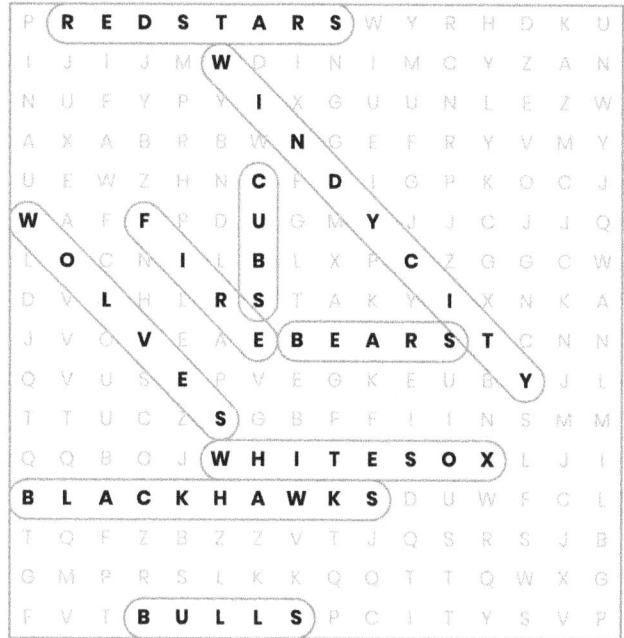

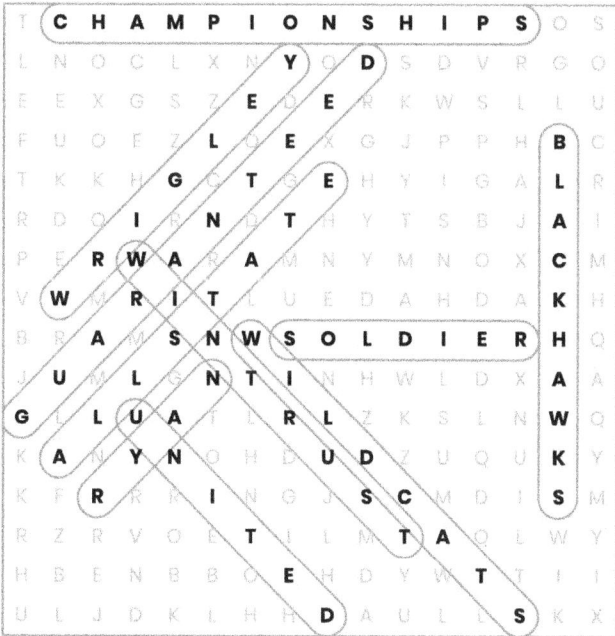

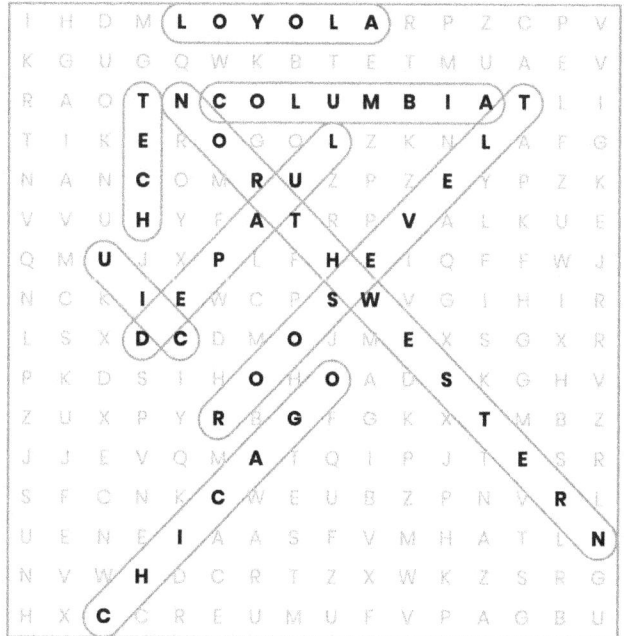

PUZZLE ANSWERS

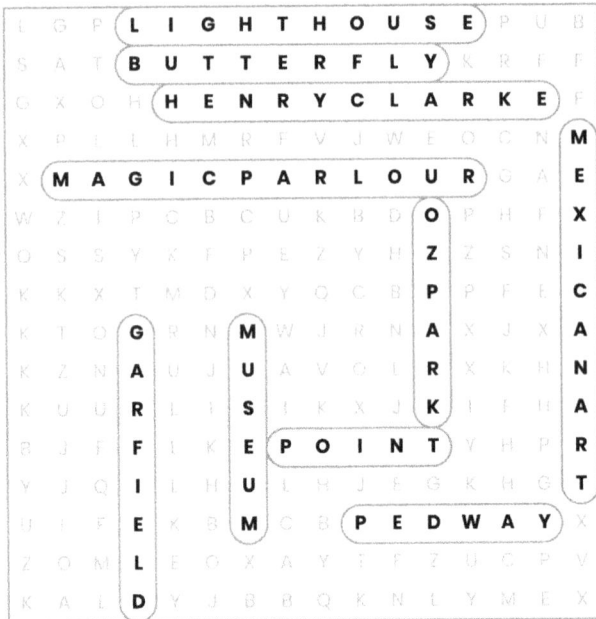

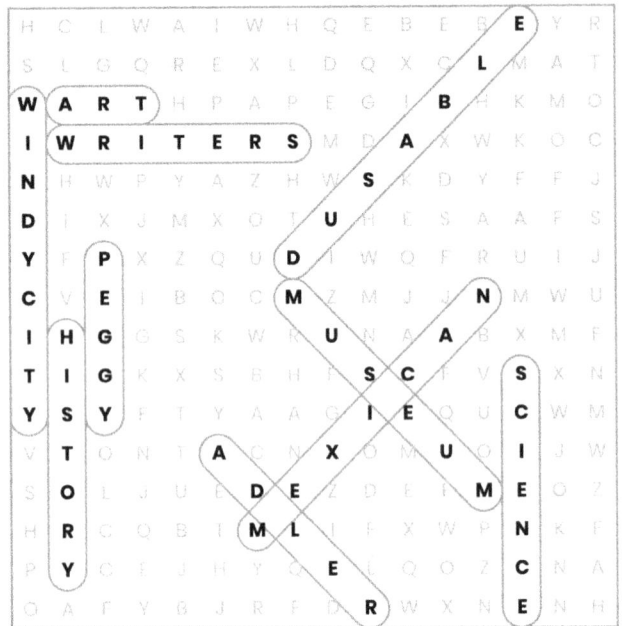

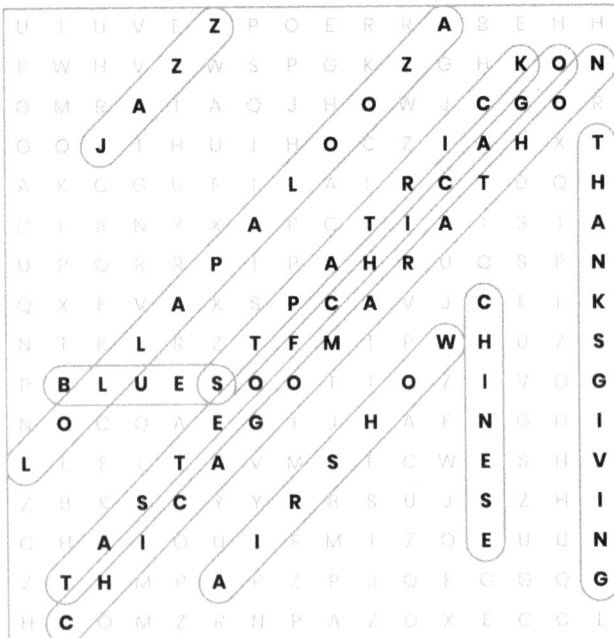

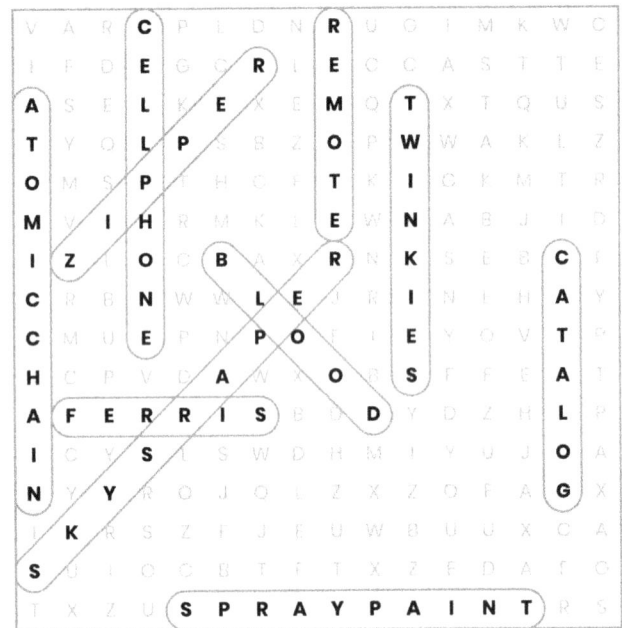

Puzzle 1:
- LIGHTHOUSE
- BUTTERFLY
- HENRYCLARKE
- MAGICPARLOUR
- MEXICANART
- OZPARK
- GARFIELD
- MUSEUM
- POINT
- PEDWAY

Puzzle 2:
- WART
- WRITERS
- WINDYCITY
- HISTORY
- PEGGY
- SCIENCE
- MUSEUM
- DMUNDLER
- EXE
- ADE
- ML

Puzzle 3:
- ZZ
- AJ
- KON
- CGO
- IAH
- RCT
- TIA
- AHR
- PCA
- TFM
- WH
- BLUESOO
- CHINESE
- THANKSGIVING

Puzzle 4:
- CELLPHONE
- REMOTER
- ATOMICCHAINS
- TWINKIES
- CATALOG
- FERRIS
- SPRAYPAINT

PUZZLE ANSWERS

Puzzle 1
- FOUR SEASONS
- MOOSE
- MONUMENT
- MIRRO
- GOOSE
- FOUNTAIN

Puzzle 2 (Neighborhoods)
- WICKER PARK
- ANDERSONVILLE
- PILSEN
- LOGAN SQUARE
- LINCOLN PARK
- RIVER NORTH
- HYDE PARK
- LOOP
- DOWNTOWN

Puzzle 3 (People)
- JORDAN
- MICHELLE
- OPRAH
- WILLIAMS
- HUDSON
- KANYE
- OBAMA

Chicago

We hope you enjoyed this book!

We greatly appreciate the time you took to explore this travel journal. As a small publisher, it means a lot and we hope we are making your travels fun and memorable.

If you have 60 seconds, it would mean the world to us to hear your honest feedback on Amazon.

To leave your feedback:

1. **Open your camera app**
2. **Point your mobile device on the QR code below**
3. **The review page will appear in your web browser**

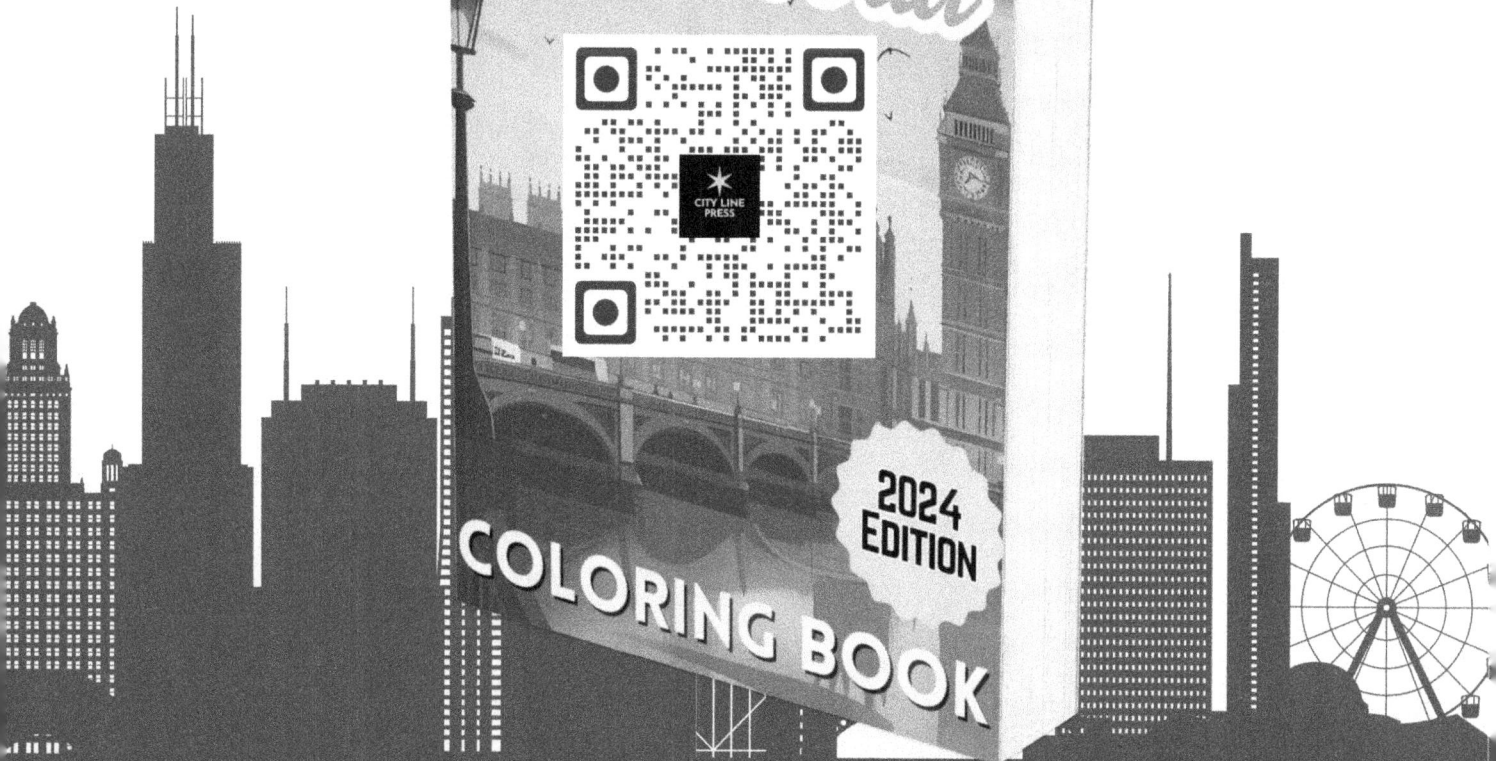

www.ingramcontent.com/pod-product-compliance
Lightning Source LLC
Chambersburg PA
CBHW081542040426
42448CB00015B/3188